Junior Science
earthworms

Terry Jennings

Illustrations by David Anstey

Gloucester Press
New York · London · Toronto · Sydney

About this book

Earthworms are interesting animals. In this book you will find out where they live, what they like to eat, how they move and how they help the soil. There are lots of different experiments for you to try. You can find out how many worms there are in your lawn, how to make a home for worms and much more.

First Paperback Edition 1990
ISBN 0 531 17501 4

First published in the
United States in 1988 by
Gloucester Press
387 Park Avenue South
New York, NY 10016

ISBN 0 531 17097 7

Library of Congress Catalog
Card Number: 87-83005

© BLA Publishing Limited 1988

This book was designed and produced by BLA Publishing Limited, TR House, Christopher Road, East Grinstead, Sussex, England

A member of the Ling Kee Group
London Hong Kong Taipei Singapore New York
Printed in Great Britain

Earthworms are small animals that live in the soil. They don't have eyes, ears or legs. But an earthworm does have a mouth, a head end and a tail end. The head end moves forward. It is also pointed.

You can have a worm hunt in your garden. Lay a sheet of plastic on the ground. Dig up some soil and search through it. Count how many earthworms there are. Then look in other parts of the garden. Make a list like this to see where you find the most worms.

	Number of worms
Flower garden	6
Rose bed	3
Cabbage patch	4
Under large stone	2
Compost heap	11
Under plank of wood	4

There are lots of different kinds of worms. There are big worms, small worms and worms of different colors. The numbers of rings, or segments, can differ. Even a small garden may have several different kinds of worms.

Worms become shorter and longer as they move along. You can see this for yourself. Find a large worm and put it on a tray of damp soil. Watch the worm moving and measure it as it moves along. The worm in the picture was sometimes only two inches long and sometimes it was six inches long.

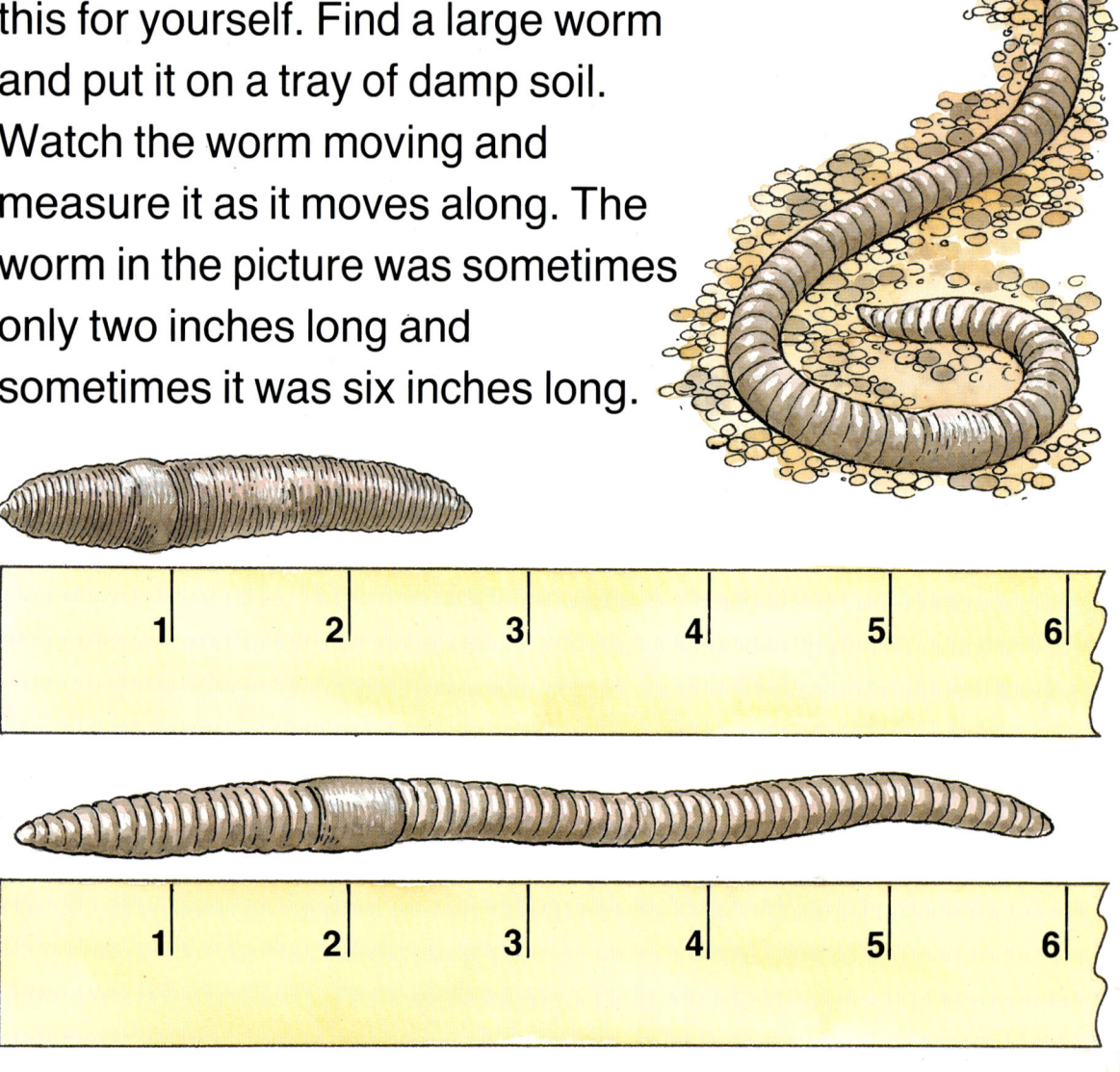

Put a worm on a sheet of paper and listen carefully. You will hear little scratching noises. On almost every segment of its body an earthworm has eight small bristles. These help the worm move along. The bristles make the scratching noises. On smooth, shiny surfaces the bristles cannot grip.

You can work out how many worms there are in a patch of grass. You may need help from a grown-up. Measure an area of grass in square feet. Mark a square on the grass with sticks so that it measures one square foot. Fill a watering can with water and water your square well. Earthworms will soon come up to the surface.

Pick up the worms carefully. Count them and let them go. They will soon wriggle away. Now multiply the number of worms with the size of the area of grass. You will then know how many worms the whole area contains.

You can make a home for worms like this. Put some damp soil in a large jar. Then put some damp sand in the jar. Next put more damp soil in the jar. Continue putting different layers in the jar until it is nearly full. Put three worms and some dead leaves on top of the soil. Now cover the jar with a piece of plastic.

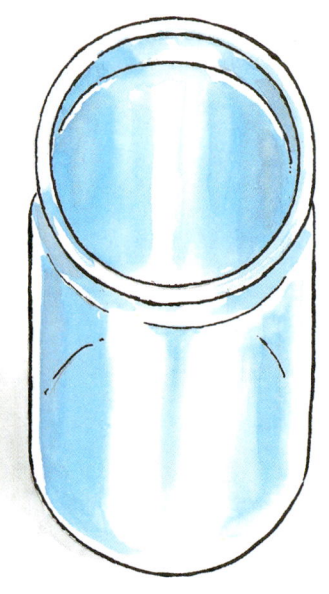

Make small holes in the plastic to let air in the jar. Then the worms can breathe. Put a piece of black paper around the jar to keep the worms in the dark. One week later remove the paper. You will see that the worms have made burrows and that they have mixed up the layers of sand and soil. The leaves have been dragged down into the burrows.

During the day, earthworms stay in their burrows. At night they come out and wriggle over the ground. If you shine a flashlight on the worms they will go down their burrows. Earthworms have no eyes They can "feel" the light shining on them because of special cells in their skin.

Dig in your garden in the summer when the soil is damp and warm. You will find lots of earthworms. But in winter when the ground is cold and frosty, there are no worms near the top of the soil. This is because worms bury deep into the ground where the ground is slightly warmer in winter.

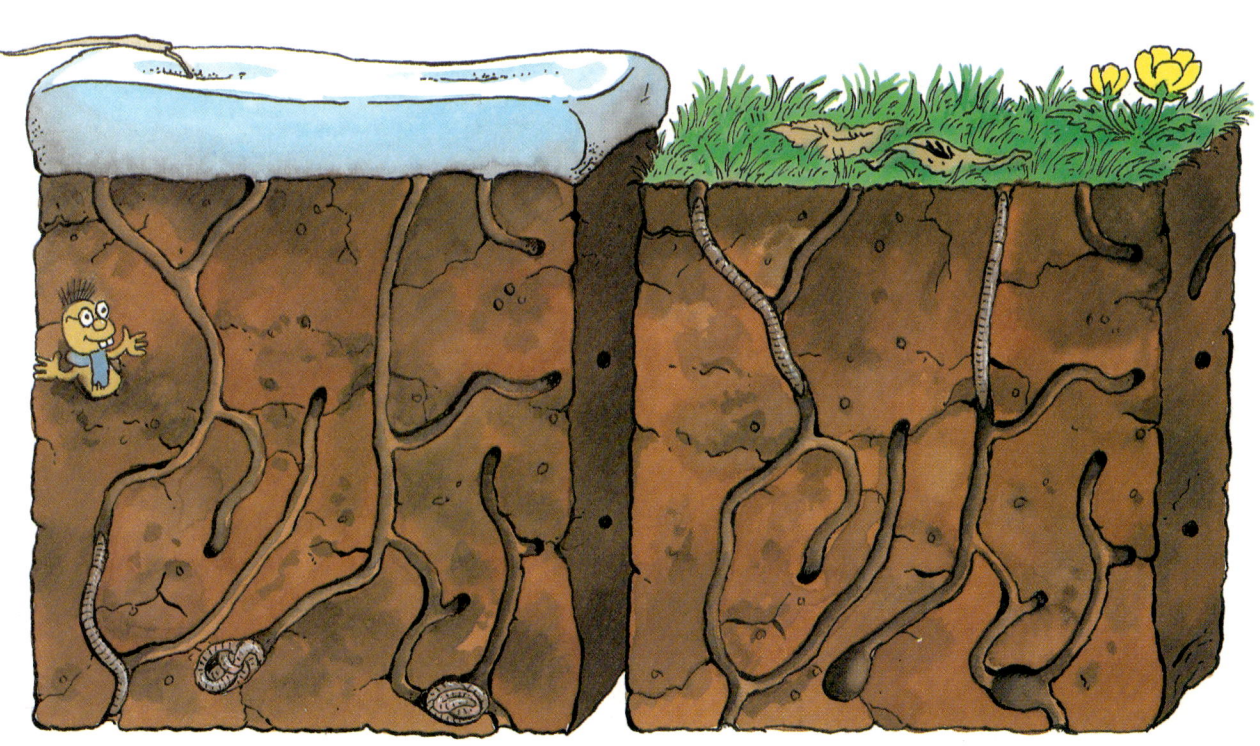

Worms like to eat leaves. This experiment shows what kinds of leaves worms like best. Fill a bowl with damp soil. Put five worms in the bowl and then cover it with plastic. Look at the bowl the next day. You will see that the worms have all burrowed into the soil.

Now lay different kinds of leaves on the bowl and again cover it with plastic. Look the next day and see which of the leaves have gone. The worms will have pulled the leaves they like best into their burrows to eat them.

As earthworms burrow they swallow some of the soil. They eat bits of rotting plants and dead animals in the soil. Sometimes they pull leaves into their burrows. The leaves rot away and the worms can then eat them.

Waste soil comes out of the tail end of a worm. This waste soil is called a worm casting. You can often find worm castings on the lawn. They show where the worms have been feeding at night.

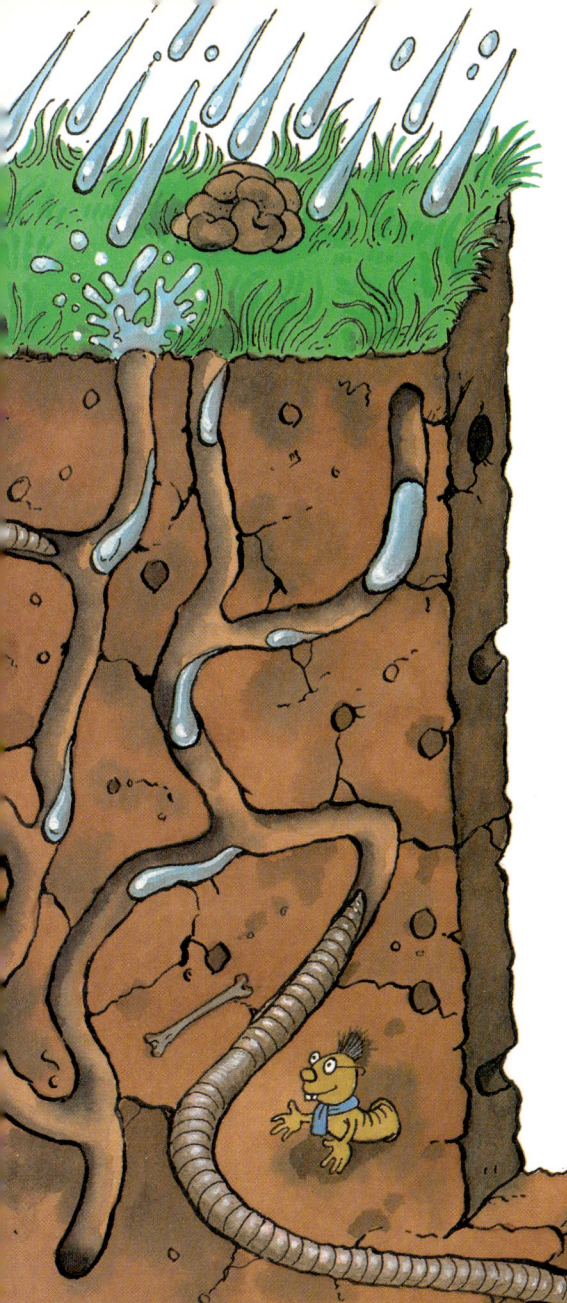

Earthworms help the soil in many ways. They eat up dead plants and animals. Their waste is good for the soil. It makes the soil better for plants to grow in.

Worm burrows help make the soil looser. They let air into the soil. The plants and animals in the soil can breathe the air. The burrows also help rain water to drain away. Then the rain doesn't form puddles on the soil.

There are no male worms and there are no female worms. Every worm is both male and female. But two worms have to mate if they are to lay eggs. Sometimes you can find two worms joined together. They are mating.

Later both worms will lay eggs. The eggs are laid in loose soil inside a little brown cocoon. A tiny worm hatches from each egg. The young worm grows larger. One day it will lay eggs after it has mated.

cocoon

Worms like wet places best. You can see this for yourself. Mark the middle of a dish. Put a dry paper towel in half the dish. Put a damp paper towel in the other half. Put five worms in the middle of the dish.

Now cover the dish with a piece of cardboard. Ten minutes later look at the dish. You will see that most of the worms are in the damp half of the dish.

Earthworms don't like light. Put damp paper towels in the bottom of a shallow dish and place it on a windowsill. Put five worms in the middle of the dish. Cover over one half of the dish with a piece of cardboard. Ten minutes later look at the dish. The earthworms will be under the cardboard.

Earthworms need to keep their bodies damp. If they get too dry they die. That is why they live in damp soil. They must also keep safe from larger animals which would eat them if they could. Moles, shrews and birds eat earthworms. Worms hide in the ground and only come out at night.

glossary

Here are the meanings of some words you may have used for the first time in this book.

burrow: a hole or tunnel in the ground that an animal lives in.

cocoon: a case around the eggs or young of a small animal.

drain: to take away water by pipes or tunnels.

female: any person or animal that can become a mother.

hatch: to break out of an egg.

male: any person or animal that can become a father.

mating: when a pair of animals come together so that eggs or babies can be produced.

worm casting: a little heap of waste soil which has come from an earthworm's body after it has eaten.

index

bristles 7
burrows 11, 12, 14, 16, 17, 23
cocoon 19, 23
eggs 19, 23
food 16
head end 3
leaves 10, 11, 14, 16
light 12, 21
mating 19, 23
measuring 6
movement 7
segment 5, 7
size 5, 6
summer 13
tail end 3, 16
winter 13

worm casting 16, 23
worm home 10, 11
worm hunt 4